trace & Write
CURSIVE WRITING
Sentences

Published by

MAPLE PRESS PRIVATE LIMITED

Corporate & Editorial Office
A 63, Sector 58, Noida 201 301, U.P., India

phone +91 120 455 3581, 455 3583
email info@maplepress.co.in, website www.maplepress.co.in

2013 Copyright © Maple Press Private Limited
ALL RIGHTS RESERVED. No part of this book may be reproduced or transmitted in any form by any means, electronic or mechanical, including photocopying and recording, or by any information storage and retrieval system, except as may be expressly permitted in writing by the publisher.

Printed in 2023
Printed at Diamond Agencies Private Limited, Noida, India

14 13 12 11 10 9 8 7 6 5

The man is sitting on the chair.

The man is sitting on the chair.

The man is sitting on the chair.

The man is sitting on the chair.

The man is sitting on the chair.

Turn off the lights and go to bed.

Turn off the lights and go to bed.

Turn off the lights and go to bed.

Turn off the lights and go to bed.

Turn off the lights and go to bed.

3

The balloon rose quickly in the sky.

The balloon rose quickly in the sky.

The balloon rose quickly in the sky.

The balloon rose quickly in the sky.

The balloon rose quickly in the sky.

Bananas are yellow in colour.

Bananas are yellow in colour.
Bananas are yellow in colour.
Bananas are yellow in colour.
Bananas are yellow in colour.

We should brush our teeth every day.

We should brush our teeth every day.

We should brush our teeth every day.

We should brush our teeth every day.

We should brush our teeth every day.

Cats are covered with soft fur.

Cats are covered with soft fur.

Cats are covered with soft fur.

Cats are covered with soft fur.

Cats are covered with soft fur.

Carrots are very good for our eyes.

Carrots are very good for our eyes.

Carrots are very good for our eyes.

Carrots are very good for our eyes.

Carrots are very good for our eyes.

There are seven days in a week.

There are seven days in a week.

There are seven days in a week.

There are seven days in a week.

There are seven days in a week.

Animals should be treated with love.

Exercise keeps us fit and healthy.

Exercise keeps us fit and healthy.
Exercise keeps us fit and healthy.
Exercise keeps us fit and healthy.
Exercise keeps us fit and healthy.

The Earth revolves around the Sun.

The Earth revolves around the Sun.

The Earth revolves around the Sun.

The Earth revolves around the Sun.

The Earth revolves around the Sun.

Sugarcane is juicy and sweet in taste.

Sugarcane is juicy and sweet in taste.

Sugarcane is juicy and sweet in taste.

Sugarcane is juicy and sweet in taste.

Sugarcane is juicy and sweet in taste.

Most dogs bark during the night.

Most dogs bark during the night.
Most dogs bark during the night.
Most dogs bark during the night.
Most dogs bark during the night.

Lotus is our national flower.

Lotus is our national flower.

Lotus is our national flower.

Lotus is our national flower.

Lotus is our national flower.

The ostrich is the largest bird.

The ostrich is the largest bird.

The ostrich is the largest bird.

The ostrich is the largest bird.

The ostrich is the largest bird.

Cheetah is the fastest animal.

Cheetah is the fastest animal.
Cheetah is the fastest animal.
Cheetah is the fastest animal.
Cheetah is the fastest animal.

We should always respect elders.

Pandas live in bamboo forests.

Pandas live in bamboo forests.

Pandas live in bamboo forests.

Pandas live in bamboo forests.

Pandas live in bamboo forests.

Giraffe is the tallest animal.

Giraffe is the tallest animal.

Giraffe is the tallest animal.

Giraffe is the tallest animal.

Giraffe is the tallest animal.

A fish breathes through its gills.

A fish breathes through its gills.

A fish breathes through its gills.

A fish breathes through its gills.

A fish breathes through its gills.

The forests have beautiful trees.

The forests have beautiful trees.

The forests have beautiful trees.

The forests have beautiful trees.

The forests have beautiful trees.

The waiter patiently took our orders.

The waiter patiently took our orders.

The waiter patiently took our orders.

The waiter patiently took our orders.

The waiter patiently took our orders.

The mouse ran quickly across the room.

The mouse ran quickly across the room.
The mouse ran quickly across the room.
The mouse ran quickly across the room.
The mouse ran quickly across the room.

Drinking milk is good for health.

Drinking milk is good for health.

Drinking milk is good for health.

Drinking milk is good for health.

Drinking milk is good for health.

Keep your dishes in the sink.

Keep your dishes in the sink.

Keep your dishes in the sink.

Keep your dishes in the sink.

Keep your dishes in the sink.

A jug is used for storing water.

A jug is used for storing water.

A jug is used for storing water.

A jug is used for storing water.

A jug is used for storing water.

Every day the Sun rises in the east.

An octopus has eight arms.

An octopus has eight arms.

An octopus has eight arms.

An octopus has eight arms.

An octopus has eight arms.

The kettle whistles on the stove.

The kettle whistles on the stove.

The kettle whistles on the stove.

The kettle whistles on the stove.

The kettle whistles on the stove.

Reading books is a good habit.

Reading books is a good habit.

Reading books is a good habit.

Reading books is a good habit.

Reading books is a good habit.

Children love going to the zoo.

Children love going to the zoo.

Children love going to the zoo.

Children love going to the zoo.

Children love going to the zoo.